KEEPING FIT
A HANDBOOK FOR
PHYSICAL CONDITIONING
AND BETTER HEALTH

KEEPING FIT
A HANDBOOK FOR PHYSICAL CONDITIONING AND BETTER HEALTH

Fred Neff

Photographs by James E. Reid

Lerner Publications Company
Minneapolis

23270

*To Elliot Neff, who was an inspiration to all who knew
him because of his kindness and his love of beauty*

LIBRARY OF CONGRESS CATALOGING IN PUBLICATION DATA

Neff, Fred.
    Keeping fit.

    (Fred Neff's Self-Defense Library)
    Includes index.
    SUMMARY: Discusses proper nutrition and provides exer-
cise programs for both beginners and those more physically fit.

    1. Hygiene—Juvenile literature. 2. Exercise—Juvenile litera-
ture. 3. Nutrition—Juvenile literature. [1. Exercise. 2. Nutri-
tion] I. Reid, James E. II. Title.

RA777.N43 1977   613   75-38478
ISBN 0-8225-1157-6

Published simultaneously in Canada by
J. M. Dent & Sons (Canada) Ltd., Don Mills, Ontario

Manufactured in the United States of America

International Standard Book Number: 0-8225-1157-6
Library of Congress Catalog Card Number: 75-38478

1 2 3 4 5 6 7 8 9 10 85 84 83 82 81 80 79 78 77

CONTENTS

The models photographed in this book are Laura
Phillips, Mike Podolinsky, and Bill Polta.

INTRODUCTION

As an instructor of the martial arts, I am often asked how a person can condition his or her body to its peak of health and physical fitness. Because the conditioning process involves many factors, the question requires a detailed answer. Such factors as nutrition, dieting, weight control, and exercise should be taken into consideration. And so should things like an individual's fitness needs and the ways in which his or her lifestyle can be altered by the conditioning process. In an effort to show the importance of physical fitness and explain the conditioning process, I have prepared this book as a basic course on health and physical conditioning.

The material presented in this course is based on modern health practices and physical conditioning techniques. By studying this information and putting it to good use, you will notice a marked difference in the way you feel, in the way you look, and in the amount of energy you have. Remember that there are no shortcuts to becoming physically fit; the key to successful conditioning lies in the kind of training you do and in the amount of effort you put into it. Of course, it is also important that you enjoy the conditioning process. People who enjoy physical conditioning and regard it as an exciting challenge usually make the most progress in achieving their goals.

There are two things to keep in mind as you study this course. First, follow the chapters in order. This is because each chapter has been designed as a foundation for the next. Second, be careful not to strain yourself during your exercise sessions. Remember that it is far better to exercise a little during each session and improve slowly than to exercise too much and injure muscles.

COMMON QUESTIONS ABOUT PHYSICAL CONDITIONING

Students of physical conditioning usually have a number of questions concerning physical fitness, dieting, weight control, and other health-related topics. The questions that students ask most often have been included in this chapter.

1. Why is it important for a person to be physically fit?

The physically fit person has many physical and mental advantages over a person who is not as healthy. The most important physical advantage is that a person's internal organs and other body structures, such as the heart, lungs, and muscles, all function better. Along with improved body function, the physically fit person enjoys a higher level of energy and finds that he or she has greater strength and endurance for performing daily tasks. An improved physical condition also reduces the likelihood that disease—especially heart disease—will occur.

In addition to these advantages, the physically fit person also *looks* healthy and vigorous. He or she has a firm, trim body, good posture, and a certain grace of movement—the result of firmer muscles and improved muscle coordination.

There are also certain mental advantages to being physically fit. In general, a person's mind responds faster and functions more effectively when he or she is physically active. Also, mental attitudes, such as outlook on life, are generally more positive. This is due in large part to the fact that strenuous exercise provides an outlet for mental and physical tension. In short, physically fit people have a strong sense of mental and physical well-being.

2. Can a person become physically fit by taking a physical conditioning course like this one?

Yes. But remember that a good conditioning program combines both physical exercise and a guide to proper nutrition. You must do the exercises faithfully and follow the diet-planning information if you are to benefit from the program. Your progress will depend on several things: the kind and amount of physical training you are doing, your physical condition when you start the course, and the way in which your body reacts to training. Remember, too, that people are unique, and that they progress at different rates. It is the continuous effort that counts most.

3. How many times a week should a person practice the exercises in this book?

It is a good idea to spend about 10 minutes every day on four or five of the beginners' exercises (Chapter 2). These exercises are good for keeping the body flexible and in good general condition. The advanced exercises (Chapter 3) should be done three times a week, with a day in between to allow the body to relax and recover. Be careful not to overdo during your exercise sessions.

4. What time of the day is best for doing exercises?

No particular time of day is better than any other for exercising. People who work all day usually exercise either before breakfast in the morning or before going to bed at night. Regardless of when you exercise, be sure to make your exercise session a part of your regular routine so that it becomes a habit.

5. What is the best diet plan for losing weight?

No single diet plan will work for everyone. Each person must find the diet plan that best fits his or her individual needs. The best way to do this is to consult your doctor. He or she will analyze your needs and then prescribe a good diet plan for you. However, if you decide to look elsewhere for a diet plan, you should know what to look for. Make sure that the plan you choose takes into account your body's nutritional needs. Starvation diets or miracle weight-reducing plans do not do this. Nor do they encourage proper eating habits. Persons on those kinds of diets commonly lose a lot of weight at first but then gain it all back within a few weeks of going off the plan. A good weight-reducing plan offers sound information not only on losing weight but also on maintaining a variety of nutritious food in your meals.

6. Do you have any suggestions for helping me stick with my diet?

Following a diet faithfully is not always an easy thing to do. Here are some ideas for helping you to survive the difficult moments:

a. Think of your diet as an exciting challenge. Be determined to win out over old eating habits and to create a "new you" — someone who is stronger, more attractive, and more physically fit.

b. Set goals for yourself. Determine how much weight you are going to lose, and then work toward achieving that goal. Do not become discouraged by setbacks. If you are forced to go off your diet temporarily, get back on it as soon as possible. Remember that people who never give up usually achieve what they set out to do.

c. Form a mental picture of how you will look when you reach your ideal weight. This image will prevent you from breaking your diet when temptation occurs.

d. Become involved with projects, hobbies, or sports activities so that you will be too busy to think about food. This is especially important for the days when you have a lot of leisure time. It is during these times — especially weekends — that overeating becomes a real temptation. To avoid this, many successful dieters have involved themselves with such hobbies as painting, sculpting, weaving, knitting, furniture repair, or carpentry.

e. Know what upsets you. This is important because eating is often an escape for people who are upset or nervous. If you have a tendency to eat too much at these times, try to determine what things upset you. You can either avoid them or try to resolve them. If your mental and emotional state is causing a chronic eating problem, you should consider talking to a doctor or a psychological counselor.

7. Do you have any suggestions for helping me overcome my desire for food?

a. Drink a few glasses of water about half an hour before eating. You will then eat less food at mealtime.

b. Take only small servings of food when you eat, and do not eat quickly.

c. If you get the urge to have a snack before bed, do some exercises and then brush your teeth. These things have proved helpful in curbing the desire to eat.

1.

GUIDE TO PROPER NUTRITION

Because the foundation of good physical fitness is a balanced, nutritious diet, it is important to know what foods supply basic nutrients and how those nutrients benefit us.

Nutrients are the basic chemical elements in food that promote growth, provide energy, and are essential to the replacement of worn-out cells and tissues. Nutrients are divided into five main groups: proteins, carbohydrates, fats, vitamins, and minerals.

Proteins are essential for growth, maintenance, and repair of body tissue. They are especially important for maintaining bones, muscles, and skin. Proteins contain *amino acids*, organic substances that help the body change protein into energy. Foods rich in proteins include meat, fish, whole grains, vegetables, and dairy products.

Carbohydrates act as the fuel that provides our bodies with energy. When a person's diet contains more carbohydrates than are needed, however, the body changes them into fat. Foods that contain carbohydrates include rice, cereals, bread, sugar, and potatoes.

Fats are another source of body energy. They also help the body digest food. The body gets necessary fats in two ways. Some fats, such as butter, oil, and shortening, are added to food. Other fats are already present in food. These include the fats in milk, eggs, fish, meat, and nuts.

Vitamins are organic elements in food that are essential for growth, maintenance, and repair of body structures as well as for regulation of body functions. There are many different vitamins (A, B1, B2, B12, C, D, K, niacin), and each has a specific function. Lack of a specific vitamin in one's diet can cause disease. The body's vitamin requirements are supplied by a balanced diet.

Minerals are elements in food that promote growth and repair and that regulate body functions. Calcium, iron, phosphorous, and iodine are among the minerals that our bodies need.

Many people worry about whether or not they are getting enough of these nutrients in their diets. If they are regularly eating balanced amounts of basic foods, they should be receiving all the important nutrients required for good general health.

THE BASIC FOUR

What are the basic foods contained in a balanced diet? And what do nutritionists consider to be adequate daily requirements of these foods?

To provide a guide for easy diet planning, nutritionists have grouped food into basic categories. The following four categories are known as the "Basic Four" food groups. Nutritionists have arranged them largely according to the nutrients they possess. By selecting items from each group and by including them in your daily diet, you can create meals that are balanced, nutritious, attractive, and tasty.

Meat Group

When we eat meat, we are eating the flesh and body tissue of a variety of animals. Cows, pigs, lambs, and poultry provide us with the meats most common to our diets—beef, pork, lamb, chicken, and turkey. Another common food in the meat group is fish and other seafood, including shrimp, lobster, clams, and oysters. We also eat such game animals as duck, rabbit, deer, and pheasant. Other foods included in the meat group are eggs, dried peas and beans, and nuts. All of these foods are rich in proteins, vitamins, minerals, and fats. Nutritionists recommend one or two servings from this group every day.

Breads and Cereals

All the foods made from grains (wheat, oats, rye, rice, corn, etc.) are included in this group. These foods would include breads, breakfast cereals, rice dishes, and corn products. Macaroni and spaghetti noodles are also made from grain. Grain foods are rich in carbohydrates, vitamins, and minerals. Nutritionists recommend four servings from this group daily.

Even though nutritious food is important for health, it is not a good idea to eat only certain kinds of nutritious foods or to eat them in large amounts. Too much of even a good thing can cease to be beneficial if not taken in moderation. Remember that only a *balanced* diet can benefit health, and that a balanced diet involves a variety of foods.

Milk and Milk Products

These foods include milk, cream, butter, margarine, cheese, cottage cheese, and ice cream. Dairy products are rich in protein and important vitamins and minerals. Children should have three to four cups of milk every day, and adults should have at least two cups of milk every day.

Fruits and Vegetables

This food group includes all fruits and vegetables. In addition to providing essential vitamins and minerals, fruits and vegetables also provide fiber and bulk—food material that, when digested, helps the body to eliminate waste normally. We eat parts of plants, such as seeds, leaves, nuts, stems, and stalks, for fiber and bulk. In addition, the outer skin, or peel, of fruits and the tough, fibrous strands and connective tissue in both fruits and vegetables provide fiber and bulk. Nutritionists recommend one or more servings from this group daily.

2.

A BEGINNING PROGRAM OF EXERCISE

In order to be physically fit, a person must condition his or her body through exercise. Whether this is accomplished through daily sports activities or through a program of body-conditioning techniques, exercise is as important to the human body as good nutrition.

This chapter presents a program of exercise for beginning physical conditioning students. There are six sections in the chapter, and each one contains exercises for a certain area of the body. You should start by choosing one exercise from each section and practice those exercises daily for about 10 minutes. As the exercises become familiar, you can add some of the others to your program. In this way, you can create a conditioning program that will meet your personal needs.

Wear loose, comfortable clothing when you exercise so that you can move freely. And remember to exercise slowly so you do not strain muscles that are not yet strong and flexible.

BREATHING EXERCISES

The exercises in this section are useful for developing better breath control. The person who has good breath control has a lot of energy and endurance.

The Basic Breathing Exercise

Stand erect with your feet spread slightly apart and your arms hanging loosely at your sides. Take a deep breath, tilt your head back, raise your arms above your head, and rise up on your toes. Hold your breath for a count of three, then exhale and return to your original position. Repeat the exercise five times.

The Beginning Deep-Breathing Exercise

Stand erect with your feet together and your arms hanging loosely at your sides. Bring your palms together in front of your body, inhale, hold for a count of three, and exhale. Take another deep breath and raise your arms above your head. Now bend forward and exhale as you touch your toes. (Remember to keep your legs straight as you touch your toes.) Repeat this exercise three times.

EXERCISES FOR THE NECK

The Neck Stretch to the Side

Stand erect with your feet spread slightly apart and your arms hanging loosely at your sides. Tip your head to one side and try to touch your ear to your shoulder. Then tip your head to the other side and touch that ear to your shoulder. Return to your original position and repeat the exercise three more times.

The Neck Turning Exercise

From an erect stance, turn your head as far as you can to one side. Then turn it as far as you can to the other side. Relax and repeat the exercise two more times.

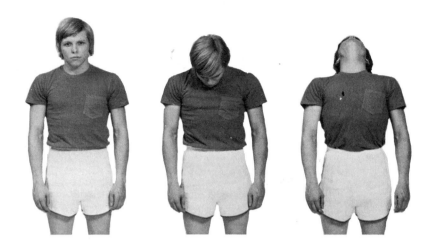

The Basic Neck Flexibility Exercise

From an erect stance, tilt your head so that your chin rests on your chest. Then move your head backward as far as possible. Return to your erect stance and repeat five more times.

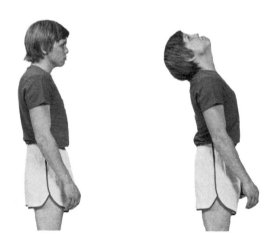

The General Neck Conditioner

Start from an erect stance with your feet spread slightly apart. Tilt your head back, tense your neck muscles, and clench your teeth. Relax and then repeat the exercise two more times.

The Basic Bridge Exercise

For this exercise, use a mat, a pillow, or a towel to cushion your head. Start in a kneeling position with your head resting on the mat. Place your hands near the mat, palms down, to balance your body. Now raise your knees off the ground and straighten your legs. In this position, turn your head from side to side and count to 20. Do not overdo. After the count, return to your original position.

The Back Bridge

When doing this exercise, always use a mat or cushion for your head. Start in a horizontal position with your upper back and your feet resting on the ground and your hips raised. To support your body, extend your arms out to either side, palms down. Now push down with your feet and arch your body. By doing this, you will be shifting your weight from your shoulders to the top of your head. Hold this position for a count of 10 and then relax. Do this exercise only once during your exercise session.

Push-Pull Neck Exercises

Stand erect with your feet spread slightly apart. Place the tips of your fingers against your forehead and push backward. Oppose the movement with your neck muscles. Now place both hands behind your head and push forward. Oppose the movement with your neck muscles.

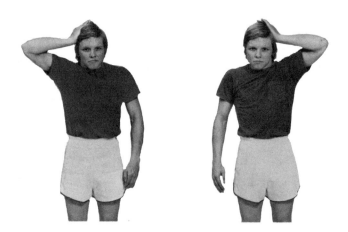

Place your right hand on the side of your head and push. Oppose the movement with your neck muscles. Now place your left hand on the side of your head and push. Oppose the movement with your neck muscles.

Do both of these exercises two times.

EXERCISES FOR THE ARMS AND CHEST

The Basic Reaching Exercise

Start from an erect stance with your feet slightly apart. Hold your arms at waist level with your hands open. Reach upward as high as you can and bring your hand down as though you were pulling something. Repeat the exercise three times with each hand.

The Arm Circle Exercise

Stand erect with your feet spread slightly apart and your arms held straight out to either side, palms open. Keep your arms straight and move them around in small circles. Move your arms forward for a count of 20. Then move them backward for a count of 20.

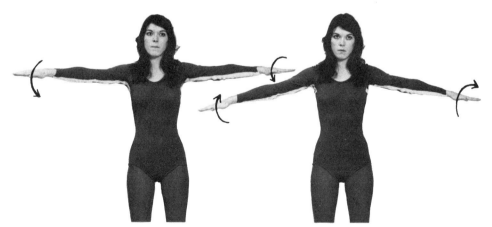

The Basic Push-Up Exercise

Start from a horizontal position, face down. Your body should not be touching the ground except for your toes and hands, which should carry your body weight. Keeping your legs and trunk straight, raise your body by straightening your arms. Then lower yourself to the floor. Do this three to five times nonstop. Push-ups will greatly strengthen your arm and chest muscles.

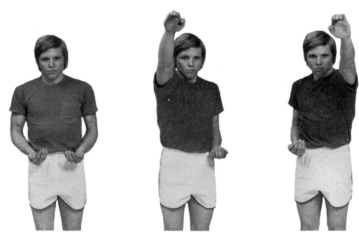

Forward Arm Exercise

Stand erect with your feet spread slightly apart. Cup your hands and hold them at waist level. Raise one arm and reach forward. Return the arm to waist level, and repeat the exercise with the other arm. Each arm should reach forward 10 times.

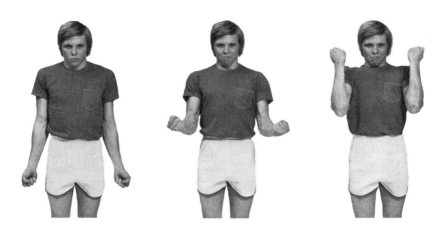

The Basic Arm-Lifting Exercise

Stand erect with your feet spread slightly apart. Your arms should be held straight down at your sides, and your hands should be made into fists, palms facing forward. Holding your elbows close to your sides, tense your muscles and raise your forearms as though you were lifting a heavy object. Raise your arms to shoulder level, and then lower them in the same way. Do this exercise once during your exercise session.

Muscle Tension Exercise

Place your right fist against the palm of your left hand and push with all your strength. Your left arm should resist the push of your right arm. Repeat with the opposite fist. Do this exercise only once during your exercise session.

EXERCISES FOR THE STOMACH, WAIST, AND HIPS

The Basic Limbering Exercise

Sit on the ground with your legs spread wide apart. Reach across your body with one arm and, without bending your knees, touch the toes of the opposite foot. Repeat the movement with the other arm. Touch each foot three times.

The Basic Sit-Up

Lie flat on the ground and, without bending your knees, sit up and touch your toes. Lie down again and repeat the exercise 10 times without stopping.

The Basic Downward Stretch

Stand erect with your feet spread wide apart. Keep your legs straight as you bend down and touch one hand to the toes of the opposite foot. Return to your standing position, and then repeat the procedure with the other arm. Touch each foot five times.

Front Bending Exercise

From an erect stance, bend down and touch the ground with the palms of your hands. Keep your legs straight as you do so. Repeat the exercise five times.

The Basic Double-Leg Raise

Lie flat on the ground and fold your arms under your head. Keep your legs straight and raise them about two feet off the ground. Hold that position for a count of 20. Then lower your legs to a position three inches (7.5 centimeters) from the ground. Hold that position for a count of 10, and then relax. Repeat this exercise twice.

The Basic Side Stretch

Spread your legs about 8 to 10 inches (20-25 centimeters) apart. Place your left hand on your hip and stretch to the left as far as you can. Repeat on the right side. Stretch to each side three times.

The Body Circle Exercise

Stand erect with your feet wide apart and your hands on your hips. With your feet planted firmly, bend to the right and rotate the upper half of your body backward in a full circle. Repeat the same circular movement to your left. Do this exercise once during your exercise session.

The Body Twisting Exercise

Spread your legs apart, bend your knees, and hold your arms straight out to either side. Twist at the waist as far as you can in each direction. Twist to each side three times.

LEG EXERCISES

The Basic One-Leg Stretch

From a squatting position, extend one leg out to the side. With your hand, gently push down on the upper part of the leg. Repeat with the other leg. Do this exercise once during your exercise session.

The Rising Exercise

Stand erect with your feet together and your arms hanging loosely at your sides. Rise up on your toes and hold the position for a count of three. Repeat five times.

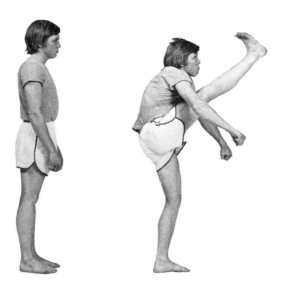

The Leg Kick Exercise

Start in a relaxed stance with your feet together. Kick one leg and then the other straight up without bending your knees. To benefit fully from this exercise, you must kick as high as possible. Repeat the exercise five times.

The Basic Two-Leg Stretch

Stand erect with your feet spread slightly apart. Then slowly spread your legs farther apart and lower yourself to the ground. The basic two-leg stretch should be learned gradually so that leg muscles are not damaged. Do it only once during each exercise session.

EXERCISES FOR THE BACK

The Basic Back-Pull Exercise

Stand erect with your feet spread slightly apart. Hold your hands loosely at your sides with the palms open and facing forward. Keeping your legs straight, bend down and clasp the backs of your legs with your hands. Pull down on your legs for a count of three, and then return to your original stance. Repeat this exercise five times.

The Basic Back-Stretching Exercise

Lie on your back with your knees bent and your feet flat on the ground. Bring one knee forward as close to your chest as possible. Return your leg to its original position and repeat the procedure with your other leg. Do the exercise 10 times with each leg.

The Forward-Stretching Exercise

Stand erect with your feet spread slightly apart and your arms raised over your head. Bend forward to waist level, keeping your legs and arms straight. Then return to your original stance. Repeat the exercise 10 times.

The Forward-Pulling Exercise

Sit on the ground with your legs spread wide apart, and firmly grip your toes with your hands. Now pull your body forward and touch your forehead to the floor. Hold this position for a count of five and then return to your original position. Repeat this exercise five times.

The One-Leg Upward Stretch

Lie with your knees bent and your feet flat on the floor. Bring one knee up to your chest and then raise the leg straight up in the air. Bring the knee back to your chest as you return to your original position. Repeat this procedure with your other leg. Do the exercise five times.

The Two-Leg Upward Stretch

Lie with your knees bent and your feet flat on the floor. Bring both knees up to your chest and then raise both legs straight up in the air. Bring both knees to your chest again and return your feet to the floor. Repeat the exercise twice.

The Double-Knee Stretch

Lie on the ground with your knees bent and your feet flat on the floor. Bring both knees forward to your chest. Then return to your original position. Repeat this exercise five times.

The Pressure Stretching Exercise

Start this exercise from an erect stance with your feet spread slightly apart and your hands clasped behind your head. Bend at the waist and swing your left elbow as far toward your right foot as you can. Now reverse your direction and swing your right elbow toward your left foot. Then return to your upright position. Do this exercise twice.

3.

AN ADVANCED PROGRAM OF EXERCISE

If you have faithfully practiced the beginning exercises, you have probably made good progress toward becoming physically fit. After doing the beginning exercises for a period of time, however, you will find that they are no longer as challenging as they once were. When that happens, you should add more difficult exercises to your exercise program.

This chapter contains the advanced exercises that will expand your program. Like the beginning exercises, the advanced exercises are grouped according to the specific body areas that they benefit. You should gradually add one advanced exercise at a time to your existing program. For best results, do the beginning stretching exercises every day. Do the advanced exercises three days a week, with a day in between for resting muscles.

Consistent, vigorous exercise is the key to good body conditioning, but be careful not to overdo.

ADVANCED BREATHING EXERCISES

The Advanced Deep-Breathing Exercise

Stand erect with your feet together and your arms hanging loosely at your sides. Take a deep breath, bend down, and exhale as you touch the palms of your hands against the floor. Now thrust both legs behind you so that your body is supported on your hands and toes. From this position, lower yourself to the floor. Push your body up again and bring your left knee forward. At the same time, lift your head and take a deep breath. Exhale as you bring both feet together. Then return to your original position. Do this exercise once during your exercise session.

a   b   c

d

e

f   g   h

The Two-Arm Breathing Exercise

Stand erect with your feet spread wide apart and your hands held out in front of you. Take a deep breath as you move your arms out to your sides. Exhale and bring your arms back to the front. Take a deep breath and raise your arms high above your head. Now exhale as you bend down and touch your left foot with both hands. Take a deep breath and stand straight as you raise your arms high above your head once again. Now exhale as you bend down and touch your right foot with both hands. End in a relaxed stance. Do this exercise once during your exercise session.

ADVANCED NECK EXERCISES

The Advanced Bridging Exercise

Kneel on the floor with your head resting on a mat or thick towel. Straighten your legs so that your body is arched and supported on your toes, your hands, and your head. Now fold your arms over your chest and hold that position for a count of 20. Do this exercise once during your exercise session.

The Full-Circle Neck Exercise

Stand erect with your feet spread slightly apart and your hands hanging loosely at your sides. Turn your head slowly in a complete circle, first to the left and then to the right. Do this exercise once in each direction.

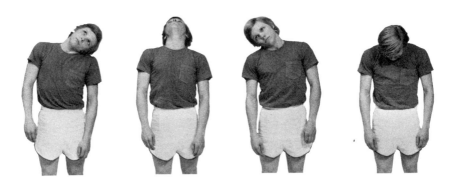

The Two-Person Neck-Resistance Exercise

Position yourself on the floor on your hands and knees. Your partner should stand in front of you and place his or her hands on the back of your head. From your position, try to raise your head against the resistance of your partner's hands. This resistance should last for a count of five. Do this exercise once during your exercise session.

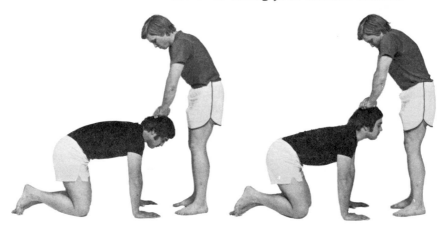

ADVANCED EXERCISES FOR THE ARMS AND CHEST
The Two-Person Resistance Push-Up

Assume the push-up position with your body weight supported on your toes and hands. Your partner should be kneeling next to you with his or her hands on your upper back. As you try to push up from the floor, your partner should resist the movement for a count of five. Do this exercise once during your exercise session.

The Two-Person Elbow-Resistance Exercise

Start in a kneeling position with your elbows extended out to your sides. Your partner should be standing behind you gripping your elbows. As you try to raise your elbows, your partner should resist the movement. This resistance should last for a count of five. Do this exercise once during your exercise session.

The Two-Person Arm-Resistance Exercise

Kneel on the floor facing your partner, and hold your arms straight out in front of you with your hands in fists. Your partner should have a firm grip on your wrists. As you try to raise your arms, your partner should resist the movement for a count of five. Do this exercise once during your exercise session.

The Upward-Lifting Exercise
From the Ground

Lie with your knees bent and your feet flat on the floor. Rest your elbows on the floor and hold a 20-pound (9-kilogram) weight in each hand. Now straighten your arms over your chest and lower them again. Do this exercise five times.

Lateral Raises From the Ground

Lie with your knees bent and your feet flat on the floor. Rest your elbows on the floor and hold a 10-20-pound (4.5-9-kilogram) weight in each hand. Straighten your arms and lift the weights over your chest. Now, keeping your arms straight, lower the weights out to either side of your body and hold them an inch off the floor. Straighten your arms over your chest again and then return them to the starting position. Repeat this exercise five times.

The Palms-Facing-Outward Lifting Exercise

Stand erect with your feet spread slightly apart, and hold a 10-20-pound (4.5-9-kilogram) weight in each hand, palms out. Bend both arms at the elbow and lift the weights to shoulder level. Lower your arms in the same way. Repeat the exercise three times. (When the amount of weight in each hand becomes comfortable to lift, increase it.)

The Palms-Facing-Downward Lifting Exercise

Start from an erect stance with your feet spread slightly apart. Hold a 10-20-pound (4.5-9-kilogram) weight in each hand, palms facing toward you. Bending your arms at the elbows, lift the weights to shoulder level and hold for a count of two. Then raise your arms over your head. Lower the weights to shoulder level again and then return to your original position. This exercise should be done five times at first and then more often as your arms become stronger.

41

ADVANCED EXERCISES FOR THE STOMACH, WAIST, AND HIPS

The Knee Swing Exercise

Lie with your knees bent and your arms extended straight out to your sides, palms down. Swing your knees to the left and touch the floor. Then swing them to the right and touch the floor. Repeat the exercise five times.

The Jackknife Exercise

Lie on the floor with your legs together and your arms above your head. Sit up and draw your knees to your chest. Hold this position for a count of two. Then return to your original position. Repeat this exercise three times.

The Advanced Sit-Up

Lie with your legs together and your hands clasped behind your head. Sit up and touch your right elbow to your left knee. Lie down again. Then sit up and touch your left elbow to your right knee. Touch each knee 10 times without stopping to rest.

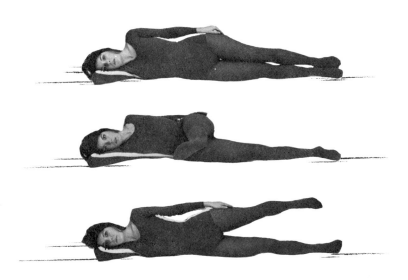

The Side Swing Exercise

Lie on your side with your forearm cushioning your head. Swing your top leg as far forward as you can and then as far backward as you can. Return to the starting position. Now roll over to the other side of your body and repeat the exercise. Do this exercise five times on each side of your body.

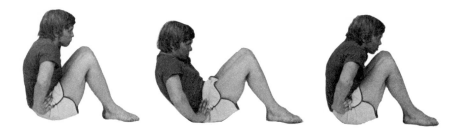

The Advanced Stomach Conditioning Exercise

Sit with your hands on your hips, your knees bent, and your feet flat on the floor. Now lean back as far as you can without losing your balance. Keep your back straight and do not lie down. When you have leaned back as far as you can, slowly return to the original position. Repeat the exercise three times.

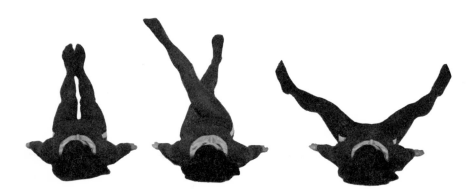

The Scissor Exercise

Lie with your hands flat on the floor and your legs raised several inches off the floor. Slowly cross one leg over the other as far as you can. Then stretch your legs apart as far as you can. Return to your original position, keeping your feet raised. Make sure that neither leg touches the floor while you do the exercise. The scissor exercise should be practiced continuously for at least one minute. Do it once during your exercise session.

The Rising Knee Exercise

Lying flat, slowly lift both legs several inches off the floor. Now bend your left knee and bring it back as close to your chest as possible. Straighten the leg again and repeat the procedure with your right leg. Make sure that neither leg touches the floor while you do the exercise. The rising knee exercise should be practiced continuously for at least one minute.

The Bicycle Exercise

Start from a position flat on the floor. Raise your legs and hips into the air, using your hands to hold yourself up. Move your legs in large circles as though you were riding a bicycle. Continue this movement for at least one minute. Do this exercise once during your exercise session.

The Windmill Exercise

Stand erect with your feet crossed and your arms held straight out at your sides. Bend to the right and touch your left hand to the floor in front of your left foot. Stand straight again and then bend to the left, touching your right hand to the floor in front of your right foot. Repeat the exercise 10 times on each side of your body.

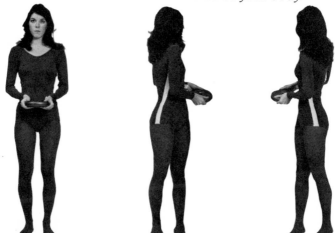

The Single Weight Twist

Stand erect, with your feet spread slightly apart, and hold a 5-10-pound (2.25-4.5-kilogram) weight in front of you with both hands. Keeping your toes pointed straight ahead, twist your body to the left as far as possible and then to the right. Twist five times in each direction.

ADVANCED EXERCISES FOR THE LEGS

The Advanced Leg Flexibility Exercise

Lie with your arms straight out at your sides, palms down, and your legs spread so that the soles of your feet are together. Bring your knees together and hold the position for a count of five. Then return to your original position. This exercise should be repeated five times.

The Inner Thigh Exercise

Sit erect and hold the soles of your feet together with your hands. Now move your knees as close to the floor as possible. When your knees reach their lowest position, hold them there for a count of five. Then relax. Repeat the exercise three times.

The Knee Resistance Exercise

Sit erect with the soles of your feet together and with your elbows resting against the insides of your knees. Slowly try to bring your knees together and, at the same time, resist the movement with your elbows. Hold this position for a count of five. Repeat the exercise two times.

The Toes-Up Leg Stretch

Place the heel of your foot, toes up, on the shoulder of your partner, who should be squatting in front of you. Keeping a firm grip on your leg, your partner should slowly rise to a standing position. As your partner rises, you will feel the muscles in your leg and side stretch. Do this exercise once during your exercise session.

The Leaping Exercise

Squat on your toes, with your hands clasped behind your back. Pushing from your toes, leap up into the air as high as you can. Repeat the exercise five times.

The Toes-to-the-Side Leg Stretch

Place the side of your foot on the shoulder of your partner, who should be squatting in front of you. Keeping a firm grip on your leg, your partner should slowly rise to a standing position. As your partner rises, you will feel the muscles in your leg and side stretch. Do this exercise once during your exercise session.

The Single Leg Lift

Lie with your legs together and with 5-10-pound (2.25-4.5-kilogram) weights strapped to your ankles.* Lift your left leg several inches off the floor and hold for a count of five. Repeat the same procedure with your right leg. This exercise should be done three times with each leg.

The Double Leg Lift

Lie with your legs together and with small weights strapped to your ankles.* Lift both legs several inches off the floor and spread them wide apart. Hold this position for a count of five. Then bring your legs together again and lower them to the floor. This exercise should be repeated five times.

*NOTE: Leg weights can be purchased from any sporting-goods dealer.

ADVANCED EXERCISES FOR THE BACK
The Upper-Body Lifting Exercise
   Lie face down with your hands clasped across your back and with your legs spread apart. Raise your chest as far off the floor as you can. Then relax. Repeat the exercise five times.

The Advanced Front-Bending Exercise
   Start in an erect stance, with your feet spread apart and your hands clasped behind your body. Slowly bend forward as far as possible. Then return to your original position. This exercise should be repeated five times.

The Advanced Back-Stretch Exercise

Lying face down on the floor, reach back and grasp your feet. Now pull your legs forward and lift your head as far back as you can. Then relax. Repeat the exercise five times.

The Extended-Leg Exercise

Stand erect, with your feet together. Now lean forward and extend one leg straight back. Spread your arms straight out to your sides for balance. Hold this position for a count of 10, and then return to your original position. Repeat the procedure with your other leg. Do this exercise once during your exercise session.

4.

PHYSICAL ACTIVITIES FOR IMPROVING GENERAL HEALTH

The previous chapters have introduced a variety of exercises for physical fitness. Other activities, however—such as individual and team sports—also require strenuous exercise. We all participate in these activities more for enjoyment than exercise. But the physical exertion they require actually enhances and completes the conditioning work begun by a basic exercise program.

The activities outlined below are just a few of the convenient, inexpensive ways to keep in good physical condition. You will find that regular participation in one or more of these activities will greatly improve your general health and physical condition.

Walking is a convenient form of exercise that affects a person's muscle strength, posture, and lung capacity. Walking, especially brisk walking, also provides a valuable outlet for nervous energy. Many people have found that taking a short walk at the end of a busy day is a good way to relax.

Swimming increases a person's lung capacity and exercises the heart, circulatory system, and muscle groups. Swimming also provides a soothing massage that is good for relieving occasional body aches. Lower back pain is a common ailment that can often be relieved by swimming.

Jogging is another vigorous activity for maintaining physical fitness. Through jogging, lung capacity is increased, and the muscles of the legs, stomach, and shoulders are strengthened. Jogging also raises a person's energy level and increases physical endurance.

Bicycling is perhaps the most popular way to keep oneself in condition. Its benefits include stronger leg, stomach, arm, and back muscles, increased lung capacity, and a stronger heart and circulatory system.

INDEX

weight twist, 46; sit-up, advanced, 43; stomach conditioning, advanced, 44; windmill, 46

legs, exercises for:
    beginning: leg kick, 29; one-leg stretch, basic, 28; rising, 28; two-leg stretch, basic, 29
    advanced; double leg lift, 50; inner thigh, 47; knee resistance, 48; leaping, 49; leg flexibility, advanced, 47; single leg lift, 50; toes-to-the-side leg stretch, 49; toes-up leg stretch, 48

meat group, 12
milk and milk products group, 13
minerals, 11

neck, exercises for:
    beginning: bridge, back, 19; bridge, basic, 19; general neck conditioner, 18; neck flexibility, basic, 18; neck stretch to the side, 17; neck turning, 17; push-pull neck exercises, 20
    advanced: bridging, advanced, 37; full-circle neck, 37; two-person neck-resistance, 38
nutrients, 11, 12, 13
nutrition, guide to, 11-13

physical conditioning programs, 8
physical fitness, importance of, 8
proteins, 11

resistance exercises: knee resistance, 48; muscle tension, 23; push-pull neck exercises, 20; two-person arm-resistance, 39; two-person elbow-resistance, 39; two-person neck-resistance, 38; two-person

resistance push-up, 38

stomach, exercises for:
    beginning: body circle, 27; body twisting, 27; double-leg raise, basic, 26; downward stretch, basic, 25; front bending, 25; limbering, basic, 24; side stretch, basic, 26; sit-up, basic, 24
    advanced: bicycle, 45; jackknife, 42; knee swing, 42; rising knee, 45; scissor, 44; side swing, 43; single weight twist, 46; sit-up, advanced, 43; stomach conditioning, advanced, 44; windmill, 46

vegetable group, 13
vitamins, 11

waist, exercises for:
    beginning: body circle, 27; body twisting, 27; double-leg raise, basic, 26; downward stretch, basic, 25; front bending, 25; limbering, basic, 24; side stretch, basic, 26; sit-up, basic, 24
    advanced: bicycle, 45; jackknife, 42; knee swing, 42; rising knee, 45; scissor, 44; side swing, 43; single weight twist, 46; sit-up, advanced, 43; stomach conditioning, advanced, 44; windmill, 46
weight control, 9, 10
weights, exercises using: double leg lift, 50; lateral raises from the ground, 40; palms-facing-downward lifting, 41; palms-facing-outward lifting, 41; single leg lift, 50; single weight twist, 46; upward-lifting exercise from the ground, 40